YOU MIGHT BE A WITCH

TEDDY BOY
& the
WITCH

YOU MIGHT BE A WITCH

Understanding a Modern-Day Witch and Considering the Magick in Your Own Life

Written by Nikki Wardwell Sleath

Copyright © 2017 Nikki Wardwell Sleath

All rights reserved. This book may not be reproduced, in whole or in part, in any form or by any means electronic, mechanical or otherwise now known or hereafter invented, without written permission from the author, Nikki Wardwell Sleath.

Disclaimer: The information contained in this book is for educational consideration only and is in no way professional, social, spiritual or psychiatric advice of any kind. Nikki Wardwell Sleath and Wardwell Books are not responsible for your personal choices, your spiritual path, or the consequences of your actions.

Dedication

This book is dedicated to my husband, Duane, who has always helped me to find the courage and the freedom to follow my magick.

Acknowledgments

I would like to acknowledge the members of my amazing coven, occult order, and magickal community, the Society of Witchcraft and Old Magick. The support of all of you has been a force that truly allows me to follow my heart and put the best aspect of myself out there for the world to see. I never imagined that such friendship, connection and depth of magick was possible, and I thank every member for their contribution.

In addition to my husband Duane, to whom this book is dedicated, I would like to express deep love and thanks to my children for simply being amazing, and respecting my ways and all that I do. You have been shining examples of strong individuality, expertly handling all the skepticism and questions about witchcraft that have come your way over the years.

I would like to thank my brother, Ry Wardwell, for his amazing photographic talent, which can be witnessed in part on the cover of this book.

Lastly, I would like to express gratitude for the perpetual presence of the Irish Goddess, The Morrigan, in my life. For as long as I am worthy, I will continue to walk your names, your ways and your stories through my world.

Contents

Part 1- Comparative Memoir

Introduction

The Childhood and Teenage Years

The Young Adult Years

Adulthood: From Training to Teaching

Adulthood: Society of Witchcraft and Old Magick

Part 2- Understanding the Basic Concepts of Modern Day Witchcraft

What Makes a Person a Witch?

How Others Respond to You

What Do Modern Day Witches Believe and Practice?

How to Speak to Skeptics About the Craft

Are You a Witch? Take the Quiz and Consider!

Parting Words

Part 1

Introduction

I did not grow up with any exposure to living a magickal lifestyle, and yet I ended up essentially running a real-world school of witchcraft training for serious and talented adults. I have made a career out of teaching magick professionally, becoming the High Priestess of an amazing coven and traditional occult training order, doing professional tarot readings, shamanic healing work, evil eye removals, exorcisms, house clearings, dream work and much, much more. These are the things in my normal day to day routine.

The text messages I receive usually include things like "I found a heron skull, do you want it?", "What does it mean if I keep seeing Thor in my dreams?", "Thanks for the healing you did on me last night in the dream time!", or "My sister needs an evil spirit exorcised from her…can you do it?". In my current adult life, on the threshold of 44 years old I know a lot of Witches, Pagans, Heathens, Shamans, Magicians, Druids, Warlocks and other magical people. I read their descriptions of childhood which often talk about a mother, aunt, grandmother or other friend or relation who would teach them about herbal healing, card reading, about the magic of stones, or energy, or fairies, or dreams. Even more intriguing are the stories of all out familial witchcraft, where the Craft has been taught and handed down consistently from one generation to the next as a tradition, as a lifestyle. I never knew or had any of that. But I am not making this contrast to complain in any way about my childhood- I had a wonderful, normal suburban American upbringing for which I am incredibly grateful.

I bring up this comparison, though, to make the point that magick often exists in ways we don't realize, and for some people there may be a dormant thread of magick that is already there inside, waiting to be exposed and put to use, to bring the full richness of life into the light. You, like me, may have a strong ability to create and live in a completely enchanted worldview. You may have always had this tendency and not really known it. Or just maybe you are reading this book because you really do know it. This combination memoir and introduction to magick and witchcraft is intended to help you to learn from my experiences, and to provide you with an opportunity to peruse and compare to your own background, personality, and history for signs of magick. It is also intended to provide inspiration and help you to notice magick in your present life, and to help you learn not to miss out on magickal experiences and opportunities as they arise. It is intended to help you understand deeply that life is magickal and anything is possible.

Because this is not an instruction manual for already established witches, I also hope that this book will be recommended to people who might still be holding onto fear or a lingering negative connotation about witches and witchcraft. I hope that in describing my experiences, my practices, my beliefs and my goals and how I came to them, that more positive light will be shed upon the reality of this form of spiritual practice in the modern day.

The Childhood and Teenage Years

I grew up in the suburbs of Boston in what would be seen as a very typical American family. We had a small yard in a nice neighborhood with sidewalks and pretty, old Victorian houses. I lived with my parents and my two younger brothers and a standard rotation of cats and dogs. I walked to school, took dancing lessons, went to birthday parties, rode a bike, played hide and seek. Nothing that happened to me during childhood seems extraordinary in terms of life circumstances, but looking back, I can remember a bunch of experiences that were probably of a supernatural etiology.

I do remember always having numerous experiences of the "deja-vu" variety. I would suddenly feel as if reality had shifted, a sense of disorientation for a moment that seemed to be two worlds coming together in an unexpected way. I would feel a chill of energy through my body, a sudden increase of awareness of my surroundings, and then watch what was happening, knowing how it would go because somewhere, outside of time as we know it, I had already seen it before. I would have this happen regularly, and in a wide variety of situations. It would happen during a simple, mundane conversation with another person, and it would happen when driving to a new and different place where I had never been before. My mother did have a general interest in the concept of ESP, and we would occasionally joke or wonder together about this when I would tell of my deja-vu scenarios, but I never explored it in any real depth back then.

As a child, I always naturally believed in omens and signs, and I don't think I had any particular source for this information or for developing this belief system. I clearly remember looking out the kitchen window and using it as my own little divination practice. I would ask myself a question such as "Does [some boy in school] like me?" I would have had a predetermined idea of how I would get the answer. Sometimes I would decide that after posing the question, if a robin were to land in the yard within my view within 11 seconds, the answer was yes. If not, then no. This must have worked well enough, and consistently to satisfy me, because I used this or a very similar method ongoing for a long time.

I should also mention that I considered 11 my lucky number for a quite a number of my childhood years. This stemmed from an experience that happened when I was 6. I was in my first-grade classroom, and it was near the winter holidays. We had all colored pictures of angels, and our teacher, who I adored, had made one too. Hers, of course, looked like a Rembrandt compared to the work of all of the rest of us who were still learning simply to stay within the lines. Her angel had brilliant colors, and shading for effect, and to my six-year-old eyes, it was stunning. To my delight my teacher decided to raffle off her masterpiece by having us guess what number she had written down on a hidden slip of paper. The first student to guess the number correctly would win the angel and get to take it home. Lots of students, including myself, put their hands up in the air to take a guess... but I knew the number was 11. I felt the same sense of disorientation that I would have when experiencing deja-vu, except that I also felt a surge of adrenaline, knowing I would win and that it somehow felt like cheating to have known the answer ahead of time. This is probably my oldest memory of what I like to refer to as a "psychic impulse". This is the term I use to refer to what feels like a normal thought that simply comes through, providing previously unknown information in clear form after having posed a question and cleared the mind. I had really wanted to win the picture, so I remember asking myself what number I would guess. I didn't hem and haw in order to try to make a rational type of decision- I thought of the number 11 and didn't waver in it. I remember my face feeling flushed and hot, and feeling confident that I would win, and I did. So 11 did come to serve as a lucky determining factor in many decisions and superstitions for years after that day. I still have to look away after seeing 11:11 on a clock out of superstition that if I look back again at it before it has changed to 11:12, that my wish will not come true. The experience of knowing an outcome very clearly in that way caused my six-year-old self to think there was something magickal about the number 11, but I know now that it was an ability to open to the flow of clearly channeled information that resides in me, not the number itself, that held the magick. Nevertheless, my superstitious, number-11-based divination methods that ensued for years did seem to work, but like other magickal tools and methods, the 11 was probably a simple tool for focus and confidence that continued to allow my conscious intentions to experience accuracy.

Many of my childhood superstitions thankfully were upheld and also participated in by my friends so I never felt weird in talking about them or adhering to them. They would play the clock game that I mentioned before (which I certainly did not invent but believed in heartily) with me for making wishes at any hour we stumbled on with a repeat number, and we would of course all hold our breath when driving by a cemetery in the belief that evil spirits could enter us by way of our inhale if we didn't. I think a lot of kids play these games, and I'm just glad that I didn't have anyone berating me for doing so. Even in high school I remember my closest friend participating with me in the "if this happens, then I will get my wish" game, similar to the robin-watching game I used to play in the kitchen when I was younger. We just took it to a bit more of a mature level though- we would sit on the front porch of her house which faced a relatively busy road. We would look cute and watch the cars pass and answer our intuitive musings based on how many honks we would get from the cars going by! For example, "if we get 5 honks then [so and so] will ask me to the prom"! I also remember one of those typical middle school-aged sleepover parties at a friend's house where six or so 12-year-old girls play "light as a feather, stiff as a board". Well, we did that, and we definitely seemed to be able to lift each other in the air using only a fingertip apiece!

I also used to have another form of childhood divination that I relied on, and that seemed to work well for me. I had heard of a form of Japanese weather divination where you kick your shoe off of your foot and into the air. In more recent years I found that this is an old tradition called Geta-uranai, though I didn't know these details back then. When the shoe lands on the floor, the lore says that if it falls upright, that is with the sole on the floor and the shoe facing the right way up, that sunny weather is in store. If it falls on its side, then the skies will be cloudy, and if it lands face down then it will rain. Well, caring about the sunniness or raininess of the following day only stayed with me as a game for so long, and so I extrapolated this activity to work for me in answering questions about my own life. If I wanted something to happen in my own life, I would pose it as a question. I would then kick up my shoe, and if it landed face up then the answer was yes, I would get my wish. If it landed face down, then the answer was no, it was not to happen, and if it landed on its side I took that as a sign of continued uncertainty for the time being. I had actually forgotten how often I used to play this game as a kid until just recently when I was teaching a lesson on divination to one of my witchcraft students, and we stumbled upon the story of the Japanese weather divination tradition. It all came flooding back, reaffirming the fact that my love of magick and divination started early, before I had any idea that I would become a Witch, or that it was even possible to study and practice this as a lifestyle or a spiritual practice.

The house I grew up in was an old Victorian with a big wrap-around porch complete with porch swing. It had a foundation made of actual rough rocks that flooded with water constantly, and a big old dusty attic complete with stained glass windows. We also had an old free-standing garage that smelled of must and motor oil, and a small cluster of trees in one corner of the backyard that had a certain privacy and charm to it. This little corner stand of trees was referred to in our family as "The Secret Place". I can remember spending lots of time alone, despite the fact that I had two brothers and plenty of other kids around in the neighborhood to play with. One odd thing is that I had a deck of tarot cards that looked very old and worn. I don't remember where I got them, and I lost track of that deck sometime in the teen years. When I question my mother about that now she feels certain that not only did she not give them to me, but that she didn't even know I had them. So, I really don't know how I came to acquire that first tarot deck- perhaps I found them in the attic of the house. I didn't know the card meanings or anything but I loved to play with those cards. I would sit in one of the hidden, mysterious, more secluded spots on our property- either the attic, or in the darkness of the garage, or under the shade of the cluster of trees known as The Secret Place. I would pretend to be a gypsy, telling the future with my cards. I loved the idea of gypsies with their mysterious ways of seeing, and in fact, with the exception of a couple of years of princess costumes in my very early childhood, there came a point after which I never went as anything else besides a gypsy or a witch for Halloween, and I still love wearing those costumes to this day.

A couple of other things that stand out when I think about magickal or supernatural undercurrents in my childhood relate to some experiences of sensing things that seemed scary at the time. My mother loved to camp and hike, and there were numerous times that we would hike mountain trails, especially when camping or on vacation in New Hampshire. I clearly remember certain times, when we'd get very deep into the forest, and I would be overcome by fear, sometimes to the point of making me cry. I had no reason that I could identify for it at the time. My mom asked me "What's the matter?" and I would just say "I don't know, I'm scared". Looking back, I think on some level I was sensing the immense power of nature that abounds in such rarely worn places. I always loved the feel of nature elements such as laying in grass or moss, being in trees, or by the water. I loved to be outside even in a hurricane, letting the forceful, gusty wind rush through me. But some places offered too much mystery, I think, for a very sensitive little girl. Also, we tended to frequent a very rough trail on a certain Mount Nancy. Not only was it a little dangerous at times with the need to cross ravines and rushing streams, but there were occasional old ruins from wagons and moonshine distilleries hidden in those woods.

Not only could I have been overwhelmed by the forceful energies in the darker parts of the mountain, but I could have been picking up on spirit energy or difficult emotional imprints that had been left behind from older points in history on that mountain. It is no wonder I didn't know why I was upset- pondering spirit involvement was not something that was a part of the culture of my family.

I also had several times in my childhood bedroom when I clearly heard a voice, and sometimes laughter coming out of my closet. We lived in an old Victorian, and my bedroom had a big walk-in closet with a full-sized window. The door to my closet was just to the left of my head when I was lying in bed. I definitely felt intense energies in that bedroom sometimes during childhood...and would often run and jump from across the room to get onto my bed so my feet wouldn't ever be near the edges of the bed, just in case there was something under there. I can't remember if I ever told my mom about hearing voices in the closet. I probably just kept it to myself, thinking it would not be a plausible idea for anyone else in my family to believe.

I mentioned that my childhood was very normal, and this is so true. You may be starting to think that it doesn't sound that way based on my description of my underlying intuitive and superstitious habits, but these were only things that happened in my internal life, and they weren't even that noticeable or outstanding at the time. I think many people, if they were to look back and magnify some of their childhood internal details, would find many of these same trends or sentiments....those of experiencing the subtle magick of the world. My parents are very "normal" people who did not do anything in particular to foster any love for magick or the occult. My dad was a mechanical engineer and my mom was a teacher's aide at the time, later to go back to school in mid-life to become a nurse. My father had been raised Catholic but was not religious at all and did not attend church in his adult life, except for maybe with us kids and my mom on Christmas eve. My mom was Protestant and she took me and my brothers to Sunday school at our local Methodist church. We attended regularly, and even had to join youth group and such in our early teens. I remember having some conversations with my mom about church (my brothers and I all hated it) and about God. She admitted to me once that she didn't attend church just for the religious practice, but because she really loved to sing in the choir. She did believe in God though, and I remember her once coming to tears when I admitted that I didn't know whether or not I believed in God. I do believe in God (and Goddess) now, but at the time of my teen years this ability to firmly believe in something greater was very clouded by my disconnection from the teachings of the Bible and the rules of the church. I confused the two. When I think back on it, I always felt very aware of myself and very connected to the world, but I did not know how to use this connection to become aware of my spirituality. Like many, I was provided with religious teachings that did not provide me with any real spiritual experiences. Because I never sensed any depth of connection with my church teachings I really and truly thought that I was not naturally a spiritual person, which could not have turned out to be further from the truth.

Interestingly, during high school, I once did a genealogy project for a social studies class. I studied my father's ancestry, that of the Wardwell family, for I knew that they had migrated to America from England in colonial times, and that it would be both interesting and traceable. I was enthralled with the fact that my direct eight-times great-grandfather was Samuel Wardwell, one of the "witches" who was hung in the Salem witch trials. I was excited because I knew it would make my project more captivating than most. Of course, it was obvious to me through all of the literature and accounts I read that the trials were the result of a religious panic gone wrong. All of the modern-day writings assume that the victims of the trials (maybe with the exception of the island woman Tituba) were not actual witches, but wrongly accused because of the frenzy of accusations that occurred amidst a strict Puritanical worldview. Back in high school I didn't know about modern day witchcraft as a practice or spiritual path, and I also had not dug further to find personal accounts of Samuel. Well, later in life when I had become an actual initiated, practicing Witch I did more research on Samuel. I found some descriptions of him as being luckier in gardening than his neighbors, as being able to know things from dreams, and as being able to tell fortunes with cards. At that point, I did begin to wonder if, by my standards, Samuel had been an actual

Witch. It seemed that not only did he have some of the typical talents, but I realized those are the same types of divination at which I initially became most skilled- dream work and tarot card reading... and then it felt odd, as if I were inadvertently avenging the wrongful death of my ancestor by practicing the Craft in a day and age where I could not lawfully be killed for it. But I will say more about this in my accounts of the adult years. Suffice it to say that as a teen I felt my genealogical tie to the trials was cool and fascinating, but at the time, it ended there.

Throughout my teenage years I was always what you would consider to be a good student. I was always in honors classes and got good grades, and yet I don't think I was a particularly hard-working or ambitious student at the time. I spent most of my time in dance class, and spent less time studying than some of my classmates who took the same classes and got the same grades, but I don't attribute this to intelligence necessarily or primarily, but rather to intuition and perceptiveness. During class, I had the habit of trying to sit near the front, and to pay close attention. I would take notes, though not copious ones. Looking back, I believe I had a flair for taking in the energy, antics, personality and values of the teacher. I would instinctively write down the material that I thought would be asked on the tests, and I was usually right. It's amazing how having clear and concise notes that get right to the heart of the matter help cut down on study time. It was a good thing, too, because during my teens dancing was my passion. Instead of doing varsity sports with my friends I was in a local dance school with a performing troupe. I often had classes and rehearsals every weekday from three p.m. to nine p.m. after school, so this certainly didn't leave me with a heck of a lot of study and homework time, especially if I still wanted to eat and sleep. There definitely were a couple of early high school years where I started to border on being too thin, but that all balanced itself it out by the time I got to college.

Actually, it was when I was at the University of Connecticut studying to be a physical therapist that I realized why I had been successful in my studies in that manner thus far. My good grades had continued along with me into my studies there in the highly acclaimed and sought after physical therapy program, with a similar pattern of sitting in the front, watching the idiosyncracies and points of emphasis of each professor closely, and then still consistently needing less time to study for each test than my peers. Again, this is not due to intelligence, and I don't mean this to sound hurtful to anyone, or boastful in any way….I say it to help others to recognize their own intuitive talents in case they have experienced similar patterns in life. One day, one of my professors asked me if either of my siblings would be following after me as students at this University, and if so, were they as ambitious as I was. I chuckled and said no, I didn't think either of my brothers would be attending UCONN. And then I startled him with this forthright comment that I somehow blurted out. I said to him "You know though, I have to tell you that I am actually not very ambitious. I'm just perceptive". I took him by surprise, and I think he took me by surprise by using the word ambitious, which, when he used it, highlighted to me that I was being anything but that. I felt lazy in my studies, like I was somehow cheating my way through it, even though I never, ever fathomed cheating in any way. I actually enraged a fellow student here and there by refusing to let them cheat off of me. And I realized when I said that to him that it most certainly must have sounded boastful or egomaniacal, but really, I was just being honest and admitting my actual lack of drive. I can already hear in my mind some of you who know me well as an adult saying to yourself "who is she fooling, she has loads of drive and ambition!". This is true for me now, as an adult, in many areas of my life and work because I have a sense of inspiration and connection to the Universe that I never had then. And this connection most certainly does inspire my work, my magickal practice, my desire to share what I've learned with others, and my constant need to continue to grow and learn and experience the mysteries of life more deeply. But I know now, as I discovered at that moment back in college, that as a student I definitely did not feel inspired to work overly hard at my studies and I could have put a lot more effort in, but I just didn't feel I needed to, so I didn't.

Take a moment to peruse the nature and circumstances of your own childhood. Were you prone to superstitions? Were you exceptionally lucky, or perceptive? Did you have episodes of deja-vu? Did you see or hear things that others didn't seem to? What did you fantasize about as a child? Did you have fears that others dismissed, but that felt extremely real and important to you? In my experience, these experiences shouldn't just be dismissed as having been the result of overactive childhood imaginations. Children tend to see and perceive things more easily than adults, and remembering what it was like to do this can be a means of getting back in touch with your natural magick.

The Young Adult Years

During my time at UCONN, I had one primary boyfriend for the first three and a half years of my time there. It was always an unpredictable relationship, never with reliably established commitment, and this bothered me, but still I thought I would be with this guy forever. I thought that, but then one day, all of a sudden, without too much forethought, I changed my mind. (You will find that my tendency to make decisions and not hem and haw over things started early and continued through life.) My boyfriend was two years older than me, so when I was a senior in college he had already been working in NYC for a year and a half, since he graduated. We continued to be together, and would commute back and forth, taking turns with who would travel to see the other on the weekends. One night during the week, we were chatting on the telephone, and he spoke to me in a patronizing or somewhat disrespectful way. I had a sudden realization- almost like the universe took a highlighter and connected this conversation with the many, many unacceptable conversations that had happened throughout our relationship all along. With a new surge of empowerment, I told him that I was breaking up with him. With no warning to him whatsoever that I was no longer tolerant of the way things were, I cut the cord. I told him that I could no longer be spoken to like that, and that we were finished. Angrily, he said "okay" and we hung up.

The next day I was walking across the campus heading to my first class of the day. I was still riding on the personal high of new empowerment, not even feeling sadness or loss of any kind, despite the fact that I had pictured that man as my life partner for several years. I don't mean that to sound as if I was being cold-hearted. I really just felt very clear and intuitive about my own personal needs and my role in relationships for the very first time. As I approached a large construction dumpster along my route, I impulsively reached into my purse and grabbed out the key to my now ex's Manhattan apartment. The walls of this dumpster were high, and I threw the key way up in the air so that it landed inside, knowing full well that I could never get it back. It felt amazing, and freeing, and in that moment I had a revelatory and vivid series of visualizations. I saw myself strong, happy, and rocking out an amazing life through numerous decades and ages. I knew suddenly as a deep and solid truth that I had no need of a man, or any particular romantic relationship to sustain me. I understood that my happiness did not reside in that at all. I realized that I was "the one". I integrated the experience right away and felt its importance, but I didn't realize until much more recently just how magical it was. That was a significant psychic impulse- meaning that I was able to notice and take in energetically the huge implications of what probably would have felt like regular meandering thought to most people, and to me prior to that.

The very next night, which was a Saturday, some of my good friends in the UCONN physical therapy program invited me to go out to a bar in Hartford. One of my closest girlfriends, and another guy friend from class were dating each other. They had plans to meet some older friends who had already graduated, and they thought it would be great for us to meet. I was having fun at the first joint we went to- a sports bar where we were casually hanging out, but I didn't have any interest in these new guys I had just met. It's not that they weren't cute, but developing a relationship was no longer my priority. We moved on to a dance club type setting, and we were all having fun dancing together. One of the new guys, Duane, spent a lot of time dancing with me, and flirting. I shocked myself when I ended up kissing him right there on the dance floor without having met him before that night. I was never like that, but now that I had no real vested interest in a relationship I guess I just felt free to have fun- it felt comfortable and right and I had no appearances to uphold.

I went home having had a great time, and this Duane character began persistently calling me to hang out. We went to parties with our mutual friends, we dated, hung out, hooked up. It was a super easy connection and I was just having a great time because I had no expectations of where it might go. After a number of months, Duane and I went hiking together. We were in a forest area outside of the UCONN campus, and sitting on a rock together by a stream, there was a mutually felt sense of connection and deeper bonding. This was also a psychic impulse, and Duane may not have realized that, but he certainly felt the emotional energy attached to it. Duane became emotional, expressing how he felt about our connection and I realized how vested he was. And I felt happy, and I felt love. I was not against having a long-term relationship, despite the fact that I didn't need one. But I was certainly able to enjoy and appreciate this love bond that had developed so naturally and effortlessly. I was all in, and this would end up being the man I married. My sense of independence has often been hard for Duane, but we complement each other well. And at the time when the base of this relationship was being forged I didn't know that astrologically this Sagittarius man was supposedly an ideal mate for my Gemini self, but this has turned out to be true.

When I graduated from the University of Connecticut at age 22 with my Bachelors of Science in Physical Therapy, I began working in the field of PT right away. As a younger student, when I realized I had interests in science, anatomy and health care, I assumed that when I became a PT that I would work with dancers and athletes. I had been an avid dancer myself, and I thought that I would naturally be drawn to work in this familiar arena. I was surprised to find though, that during the internship process that happened as part of the requirements to graduate from UCONN with this degree, that I loved working with elderly patients. We were required to complete three different internships in varying types of settings. I did one in a hospital setting, one in a sports medicine and outpatient setting, and then one in a skilled nursing facility for primarily geriatric patients. I hadn't had much experience with "old people" previously in my life, so this came as a bit of a surprise to me initially. Also, and very fortunately, it will come as no surprise to you to know that there was much more opportunity to work with the elderly because of the sheer growing numbers of aged people needing medical and health care. So, after I finished my internships I took a job in a facility providing skilled nursing and rehab to short and long-term patients, most of them elderly.

Despite loving the patients themselves, I quickly began to feel a sense of growing burnout from being in the field of health care itself. Physical therapists were simply expected to be "fixers", and there was a feeling of competition among my PT peers as to who had the best manual skills. You encounter a lot of dissatisfaction when you realize that simply fixing someone isn't possible in a huge percentage of the cases. I was constantly met with family members of 95-year-olds who expressed their anger and disbelief when I could no longer get their loved one to walk. I began to develop a vague sense of how unclear and how unaware of life and death most of our society is. I felt a growing sense of frustration when I couldn't be real with people about the natural decline of the aging body. It was too big of a wall of societally built up denial, and I knew that in traditional practice I wouldn't make a dent in it. I did not know at the time that I would later transition into hospice work, where I could actually work with patients more honestly, and I certainly did not know that I would end up being completely devoted to a Goddess of Death.

I was also constantly faced with a forced inability to be creative in my work, having to simply do the thing that the facility would best get reimbursed for. This, of course, stems from our insurance-based health care system. Most of my patients were Medicare patients, and in skilled nursing facilities (SNF's... lovingly referred to in the field as "sniffs") the art of collecting the absolute maximum amount of dollars for every patient has been mastered over and over again with each change to the legislation. It is the product of the system, not really the fault of the individual facilities, and there are lots of managers out there trying their best to run moral, high integrity rehab departments offering quality care... but it has become difficult for these types of facilities to stay afloat on the monies they receive, so capturing dollars is a game they have to play, often at the expense of the real needs of the patient or the creativity of the therapists. So as a therapist in this setting, we would be told how long to spend with our patients, which modalities (applied specialty treatments such as electrical stimulation or diathermy) we should try using to prolong the course of treatment, how many weeks we should keep them on their therapy program and on and on and on. These patient care details, by the way, are all things that are supposed to be determined by the evaluating therapist based on the patient's individual and unique needs. The reimbursement system, then, is supposed to pay for that care according to what was given. Well, if you always give the patient as much possible care as you can (even if they don't truly need it) then you will take in more money!

Anyway, having your work be solely dictated by money, when you originally went into a field to care for and work creatively with people, is a terrible feeling. This lack of satisfaction at work naturally led me to try to experience more satisfaction and completion outside of work. I needed to not only manage the stress of a career quickly sinking into burnout, but I also needed inspiration and intellectual stimulation, just by the nature of my personality. I have always thrived on learning and experiencing clear signs of personal growth. I began taking better care of myself, and developing good exercise habits by going to the gym with my husband Duane (then fiance). At the gym we joined, I stumbled upon my first yoga class. I really enjoyed it and right away noticed a sense of ease and flow within myself that I had not been encountering yet in my adult life. The thing that really hit me, though, was what yoga showed me about energy.

At the end of any good yoga class, it is customary to go through the traditional "corpse pose" or savasana. This is simply lying flat on the floor in a period of meditation and relaxation in order to allow the efforts of the yoga practice to be integrated within the self more fully. Very early on in my yoga experiences I realized that I could consistently control and change the feeling of the energy in my body- directing its flow, and raising up the sensation throughout myself to a very strong tingling. I still feel the magic in this to this day, but of course at this point my usage of and directing of energy through my body has extended far beyond the walls of the yoga studio and into numerous aspects of my life, my work and my magick. I constantly use physically and mentally directed energetic flow in my healing work with clients, in magical work and rituals, for the health of my family, and of course to tap into an ever-evolving sense of connectedness to the magical threads of intelligence that I have discovered to be running through nature, and all things, all people, all places, all times.

This revelation regarding energy that happened in my young twenties made me feel more aware, more centered in my experience, and there was an aspect of power and control in this ability to sense and shift energy so easily in myself. I'm not referring to power and control in any grandiose or overly egotistical sort of way, mostly in the self-empowerment sort of way. Years later, when I attended weekly yoga classes together with a good neighbor friend of mine, we got to talking about savasana on the way home. I admitted that I could replicate that amazing tingly, energetic sensation that we experienced in class at any time, just by thinking about it. My friend was surprised, but did believe me, I think.

I still meet many people who discuss energy with me but admit that they don't really feel it in their bodies, and to me that is the more difficult situation to fathom. I actually give those people a lot of intuitive credit for continuing to seek out energy work when they are not actually experiencing the sensations in the body as validating proof of its shifts. I'm so used to feeling the state of energy quality and movement in my body that I imagine not feeling that would be akin to not seeing, hearing, or tasting, but maybe even more, it would be like not feeling something when it touches you. If I tune in to noticing the energetic state of my body at any given moment, I can clearly feel its buzz. In doing this regularly it has become very easy to sense the energetic effects of other people as they pass through me, as well as the effects of situations as a whole, and also the effects of nature and the environment. Because we don't have a universal climate of teachings around things like this as we grow up in today's day and age, this amount of stimulation and sensation may be too much or too confusing for many. A lot of people who identify as empaths (people who are more sensitive than others at feeling other people's emotions and energies) are constantly trying to shield themselves from too much bombardment of energetic sensation, but personally, I don't find the experience to be overwhelming. In fact, I consider this a talent that helps me to stay very present and alert to all that is going on around me.

Anyway, with my energy sensing skills sharpening, I felt a bit of a sharpened keenness as to what was going on in my surroundings, and I began to notice a pattern of cycling psychic awareness that was either new, or had been dormant since a much earlier time in my childhood. I started noticing an intensifying love of autumn, despite my small body's generally cold constitution. I would feel super awake, energized, inspired and psychically clear in the fall, and I could feel bursts of energy move through my body. I can only describe this as feeling like a rainstick- one of those tribal-looking musical instrument tubes that has beans or something inside, and when you turn it over, you hear the sound of the beans trickling and raining down in a cascade. I started to feel this cascade of intense tingling that would quickly trickle from head to toe, especially anytime I had a really important thought or realization. My shamanic dream mentor, Robert Moss, says "With truth comes tingles", especially when he is teaching about psychic hits and synchronicities, but I did not know this at the time.

With this invigoration and clarity infusing me every fall I developed an overabundant love of Halloween that had never really been there before, at least not as standing out compared to other holidays. It took a couple of years for me to notice that I trended this way each fall, but after these couple of cycles I knew there was no coincidence and I started wanting explanations. I began to do online searches of topics like "the history of Halloween" and "the energies of autumn", and "the effects of the seasons on people", in order to see what information might be out there on this topic. These types of queries quickly led me to stumble upon all kinds of websites about modern day witchcraft and

Wicca and such, as these traditions tend to highlight Halloween and honor the changing of the seasons and all of the various vibrations that shift and cycle through the year. Up until this point I had never read about Wicca and had no idea what it was about. Like most others, if I saw a pentagram or a mysterious-looking new age book or symbol I had previously dismissed it either as negative or as being too far out there for me. But with the readings I came across I found out that there existed an entire set of religious and spiritual teachings that encompassed all of what I truly believed. It was right in front of me, loads of information and authors just waiting to explain to me that I had been wrong- I was, indeed, a very spiritual person. I just had not ever experienced a path to the exploration of the divine that personally hooked me deeply and energetically. I began to feel it just by reading about it!

Here are some of the tenets I first came across that resounded in my soul as truth: The idea that there is indeed divine intelligence in the Universe, but that its nature is a balance of masculine and feminine, not just the masculine Father-type God I had been presented with before this point. Then there is the notion that our most direct experiences with the divine are likely to be experienced through the energies and cycles of nature, and the notion that we are microcosmic embodiments of the divine that have the ability to change and mold our environments and our lives magically. These are just a few of the ideas that I came upon in those original fated days of reading and exploring. I was completely intrigued and inspired. I read accounts of modern day Witches with their dream experiences, their ESP and deja vu encounters, their passions and their dislikes and I felt I had found my people, even though they were just elusive internet-only personalities. I had a deep knowing move through me- I don't know any other way to describe it. I suddenly knew that I had just discovered my life's inspiration. It was an incredible and revelatory experience that happened all at once. I felt the nervousness of adrenaline in my chest, because I knew this was not a socially mainstream path to take, but I knew I had no choice and would have to face that eventually.

When I first had this learning experience and revelation, I was newly engaged to my (now) husband, and we were living in our first apartment that we had rented together. It was a nice spacious place that allowed us to have our two cats with us, and it had a spiral staircase leading up from the living room toward a cozy loft which we used as the office. I can still remember being up there on the computer in one of these searches in my early discovery of Wicca and witchcraft. With the adrenaline pumping in my chest and not much of an idea how he might respond, I came carefully down the spiral staircase to find Duane watching television in the living room. I stood in front of him and said "Honey, I have to tell you something." He looked up at me with alarm since I didn't usually preface our conversations so seriously. He was afraid I was going to tell him that I was dying, or leaving him or something devastating. "What is it?" he asked. My reply was "I have realized that by my very nature I am a Witch, and that this will always be true for me." I was nervous, but had wanted to be direct, clear and unwavering. I figured if he had any major issues with it, at least we weren't officially married yet, and he could get out easily if he really wanted to. "Oh, cool, okay!?" He responded very casually, as if I were strange for thinking that this was any topic that could possibly present a concern to him. He was relieved that I wasn't unexpectedly leaving him or announcing the discovery of a terminal illness. At that point, I also felt a huge wave of relief, and then directly following that, an increasing sense of hope, inspiration and knowing that I would always feel stimulated to learn and expand along this path of magickal study for the rest of my life.

Now that doesn't mean it was all sparkly and magickal right from that moment. I had a lot of fear, because I still hadn't dealt with all of the misconceptions regarding witchcraft that were actually lodged deeply within myself. I didn't grow up with anyone telling me that it was evil like people do in some religious traditions and cultures, but it was simply not talked about. It was treated more like a mysterious taboo to be feared and skirted around. Actually, I recall an odd day that would have happened several years before, when I was a college student home visiting. My youngest brother was in high school at the time, and apparently my mom had discovered that he had a book about Wicca in his room. He had borrowed it from the library, and she was concerned that it taught very evil practices and showed it to me out of concern for him. I remember not knowing much about it at the time, but responding to her that I was sure it was fine, and that he wasn't doing anything evil.

So back to my mid-twenties, here I was, now actively reading and learning about the practices of Wicca and witchcraft, feeling incredibly connected to these philosophies, feeling them integrating fully into myself, and yet not feeling able to talk about it with the majority of the other people in my life. This feels like a lie. It feels like you have something so important about yourself that is applicable to almost all of your life situations, and that when you don't say it, you are lying, or being untruthful in some subtle way. I say subtle, but it was very palpable to me. Thank Goddess I could talk to my then fiance (now husband Duane) about it, although in terms of the Craft he was simply a distant observer, so I did crave the experience of being able to talk about the philosophies and practices of the Craft with someone who would have valid interest and (hope of all obscure hopes) belief. But at least I did not have to keep my ways or my ideas hidden at home. Some people do not even have this liberty, and that is terribly hard.

My fascination and continual need to study witchcraft was what ultimately fueled my lifelong love of reading, and this happens for many Witches, because our fascination level never wanes, and we know somehow, that there is no limit to the amount we can learn or to the amount of different magickal experiences we can have. I began reading all kinds of magickal works, both fiction and nonfiction. In terms of fiction I have loved the Anne Rice "Mayfair Witches" series, the Lev Grossman "Magicians" series, of course the Harry Potter series (many witches like to scoff at works like this, implying that because they are surreal they are fluffy and silly but I am telling you that every witch likes this stuff- those people are just trying to put up a serious, more badass kind of appearance!) and many more including the more recent Diane Harkness trilogy. One of the first magickal nonfiction books that I read was "Book of Shadows" by Phyllis Curott. Phyllis is a lawyer who lives in New York, and she is a smart, well-spoken, attractive, successful woman who also happens to be a Witch, author and pagan rights activist. I was relieved to read the personal account of how she came to the Craft, what her experiences were like, and how she perceived it. She gave me, the reader, her personality in a way which I could relate and equate myself to. She allowed me to understand one capacity in which a "normal" woman in our current society could also function as a Witch. This was not a "how-to" book, it did not provide me with concrete ways to develop my personal practice of magick or anything like that, but it allowed me to feel that anything was possible for me in my studies, and that I was not weird or alone.

There were other books that I came across early in my studies- I read some of the Wicca books by Scott Cunningham, Laurie Cabot, and I took very seriously my reading of the "The Complete

Book of Witchcraft" by Raymond Buckland. This is, in fact, a "how-to" book and it teaches a lot of the basics of a Wicca-style religious practice, and gives you a format to take yourself through a solitary home initiation program if you wish. I worked through most of the exercises in this book chronologically, taking them very seriously and doing my best to acquire all the right tools, and practice all of the meditations and personal activities thoroughly. The thing is that it did seem that there was something lacking, and I could never bring myself to finish it in terms of deeming myself an "initiated witch". It just didn't seem right to me that I could just bestow this title upon myself based on book learning. From my original revelation about the Craft I certainly considered myself a Witch at heart, but I realized that I did not consider myself a Witch by title. It turns out that this is a traditional way to think, especially when it comes to established lines- covens who have successfully handed down magickal teachings and formal initiations to students over a period of time. Initiation is coveted and considered a huge accomplishment, as it takes a lot of dedication and commitment, with the traditional course of study being at least a year and a day. So, while I learned a lot on my own studying this and other works, I considered witchcraft my path yet did not feel comfortable calling myself a Witch.

When my son Aidan was a baby I remember lots of times driving around with him in the back in his car seat, using the ride as a nice way to get him to fall asleep...but really the driving for me was a seeking. I would meander around the back roads of Connecticut listening to Enya and searching for metaphysical shops or cool-looking cemeteries. I would drive through old or historic areas and notice my ability to sense energetic changes in my body. I enjoyed it, but I definitely had the sense that I was chasing a deeper sense of fulfillment and practice that I was not yet near. I was keenly aware that there were mystical experiences waiting for me, but I didn't know how to make them happen. I appeased my needs to a minimal point by keeping up with yoga and martial arts and reading lots of books on Wicca and Witchcraft.

When my son was a year and a half old we discovered I was pregnant again, and this time it would be a girl. I was so immersed in my studies by that point that I knew my daughter needed a magical name. I floated quite a few names to my husband and he didn't like Selene, Fiona, Sabrina, Aradia or some of the others I adored...but I was very pleased to discover that he and I both loved the name Bridget. I had developed a fondness for the great Irish mother Goddess Brigid, protector of women, children and childbirth, guardian of the hearth and of livestock, giver of the fire of life. We agreed that we would name our daughter Bridget. I got a small soapstone pendant with a beautifully imprinted design of the Goddess Brigid and wore it not only through the rest of the pregnancy and delivery, but for a long time after Bridget's birth as well. I had come to consider it a link to her protection through the divine feminine. Eventually, when Bridget was out of the small infant stage and had developed into a sturdy, healthy baby I began to sometimes swap the necklace out for other jewelry choices until it became just a regular piece in the jewelry rotation. Bridget has not failed to live up to her namesake, by the way. She was born an Aries (fire sign) baby and most definitely embodies the fiery spark of ambition and creation celebrated in this magnificent Goddess.

Consider the unique path that you have taken in life so far, and examine it for magickal threads. When something is right do you just know it with your whole self? Does this allow you to be decisive and confident? Have you noticed an ability to follow your own intuitions unquestionably? What experiences have you had with church, versus those in nature, and which felt more spiritually engaging? Do you notice feelings of enlivening when you read about magical or supernatural topics? Have you noticed that you can sense the quality of the energy in your body at any given time?

Adulthood: From Training to Teaching

Once my daughter was over a year old and life and work was back to a manageable routine, I began to itch for more than just reading and studying about magick. I had been continuing to read about witchcraft, to collect some tools, and to try various simple spells or methods of divination that I found described in my books. It continued to hold such allure and yet not provide me with full satiation. I needed training, and I knew it. I needed to learn skills and information that would be passed to me from someone who had already had a great depth of experience. I needed this to become more real by having it be shared with others. I began to take Reiki training classes. Reiki is a Japanese form of energy healing where the practitioner learns to provide an amplified flow of energy through the hands. I had actually never had a session myself, but I felt that knowing how to engage in energetic healing work would be a nice addition to my practice as a physical therapist, and I also knew that energetic conduction through the body was a key ingredient in a lot of magick. I loved the Reiki classes and felt very clear and more intuitive after each one.

Over a period of a couple of years I graduated through to the Reiki Master/Teacher level of practice. Occasionally during that time I would attend a "Reiki share". This is an informal gathering of Reiki practitioners of various levels who come together to practice on one another and to have that chance of receiving Reiki, since practitioners are normally giving it. I began to develop a reputation of being able to provide a "supercharge" to anyone I was working on. People noticed and pointed out with surprise that I had a very electric quality to my hands, exceeding the normal heat and mild tingling that comes along with most Reiki experiences. I didn't think too much of it, and was only using Reiki on occasional physical therapy patients, myself and my family at the time. I wasn't doing it specifically for a living and I wasn't using it for magick. This turned out to be just the beginning of a life of amazing energy experiences. To this day, I don't require that student witches take Reiki as part of their initiation curriculum, but it is highly recommended as a powerful adjunct to their personal and magickal practices. The very act of learning to conduct the flow of healing energy as used in Reiki causes the practitioner to become better and better at sensing the normal flow of energies in and around them. This causes the person to also be able to sense changes in atmosphere and circumstances that are happening in and around themselves, and they are often felt as interesting sensations in the body or the atmosphere around the body. Therefore, this relationship and confidence with routine energy flow can cause intuitions about feeling spirit activity, reading moods and energies in others, sensing trends in weather, etc, to all become more sharpened and honed. I didn't really know all of this at the time, although I did sign up for Reiki on an intuitive whim in the first place!

Also, during the summer of 2006, when my daughter was still a toddler and I was seeking for teaching and inspiration, I came across the woman who was to become my magickal teacher. I was searching on the website witchvox.com- a place where you can look up personal listings of local witches and pagans looking to connect with like-minded folks. You can also search for metaphysical shops in your area, as well as teachers, groups and covens. I noticed that there were a few groups offering witchcraft classes in my region of Connecticut, and I did a little reading about each. The one I was most drawn to was the Religious Order of Witchcraft, also known as ROOW. The listing seemed sincere and intelligent, and the coven had a lineage that had been going on for over forty years, whereas all the other groups I seemed to find appeared to be new and self-constructed. ROOW is a coven in the tradition of American Witchcraft. This is not specifically Wiccan, just as a Baptist church has different traditions from a Catholic one, yet both are Christian. Wicca and Witchcraft are both spiritual paths under the general umbrella of paganism, and they have a lot in common but are definitely not the same. I decided to undertake formal training and went on to achieve my initiation as a Witch and then a Priestess in that order.

Magick was finally seeping its way more fully into my life. Learning in a structured initiation lineage tradition is amazing, and it is hard for me to imagine a better method of magickal immersion overall- I think this is why, in lineages that have stood the test of time, the traditional "year and a day" of training required to achieve initiation is considered standard. I cannot divulge any specifics about my training or about that order as that is considered oathbound information. I can say, though, that by studying formally, I felt more and more of an innate sense of connectivity to, and an expanded view of the universe. By sharing my learning and my practice with others I gained confidence in my energetic abilities, and in-person validation of my divination abilities. That may sound very broad and cliche, but it was true. I felt super empowered by my studies and how well I was able to project energy and command space in ritual for my peers.

A couple of years after my period of training in ROOW, during the time period from 2010-2012, I earned my Masters in Integrative Health and Healing, and in doing so, gained not only more holistic expertise, but fabulous experiences and certifications in shamanic practice, hypnosis and dream work. That experience with the holistic grad school The Graduate Institute was life changing and empowered me immensely toward my ultimate role as a Witch. It was in those years that I really "came out of the broom closet" and began being very open with others about my role as a Priestess of the Craft. This led to me speaking openly about it in social media, and ultimately becoming known generally as a Witch in my community. Also, after finishing this Master's Degree, with all of the additional certifications it resulted in, I could no longer ignore the urge to start my own holistic practice.

In 2013, I started renting office space so that I could have a place to start seeing private clients for Reiki, PT, hypnosis, dream work and shamanic work. I planned to continue working as a PT in my regular corporate job 20 hours a week and take clients in my spare time, but I started acquiring private clients pretty quickly. It didn't take long before I had to stop working at the rehab facility because I no longer had time. I took on some home care clients, thinking that the flexibility of scheduling in this type of treatment would let me still have some regular income while building my business. It did, but only for about a year.

By 2015, I no longer even had enough time to allow for driving to a client's house because of the amount of appointments I routinely had on my schedule, so I had to step back from that, and found that I had successfully transitioned to working solely for myself. It was scary but also incredibly gratifying. I was getting the chance to use my magickal, energetic and intuitive healing skills with clients every day, in whatever way was right at the time. I had never had that kind of freedom before, and it felt so right, and so much like me. As I stepped into offering myself authentically to my community, I also began to teach Reiki certification classes, and individual public workshops on all kinds of various holistic and spiritual topics. I began to have access to many awesome, holistically-minded people on a daily basis.

Throughout all of this I was also becoming constantly more verbal and at ease talking with most anyone about the fact that I was a Witch. I was met with immense acceptance, and more than a little curiosity, with many people longing to learn more.

In 2014, with several people in my community making themselves known to me to be ready to train in the Craft, I decided to branch off and form my own coven. Doing this would enable me the freedom to be able to write my own rituals, customize a curriculum for my students, and provide them with proper training in whatever way I saw fit. I have always been a very individually empowered person, and often quite a loner. I am always a freedom seeker, which is why I had become unhappy in the traditional physical therapy setting and sought out holistic alternatives to begin with. I thrive and am at my best when I have complete creative license both in my work and in my spiritual practice, so starting my own unique group was the natural way for me to go.

Formal training in a lineage and initiation tradition of the Craft is not something that the majority of people who self-identify as witches get to do in their lifetime. Even so, have you fantasized about being a witch, being part of a coven, or doing formal ritual magick? What types of reading, television and movies are you drawn to? Do you find yourself looking for spiritual or metaphysical workshops? Are you the kind of person who loves to go into magickal shops, or get psychic readings? Are you excited to read further?

Adulthood: Society of Witchcraft and Old Magick

As I revamped all of my materials and got used to the ongoing routine of running my coven, I started noticing that more people in my community were beginning to speak up to me regarding their own interest in training in the coven. I realized that my schedule was already getting a little full between teaching my three current students each a private two-hour lesson per week, and fitting in my holistic client appointments with the public classes I was teaching. I could not imagine taking on any more private students. I decided then that I would move to a group class format. I would collect names of interested people and then hold a planning and information session for them where they could have all of their questions about the coven answered, and I could create a class time for all of the students still interested to start and come together at the same time every week. I would get to teach multiple people at once, and I figured it would work as long as they all kept up together with the curriculum.

Well, it did work. I had twelve new students start in September of 2015- this was two classes, or cohorts, of students, each with six students. Things ran very well, and it was a very conscientious, high integrity group of people. I moved my business into a larger space that fall, in fact, to accommodate our growing numbers. Another new group started in February of 2016, and two more new groups in August and September of that same year. By the end of

October 2016 our coven had three initiated Priestesses (including myself), seven other fully initiated witches, and 17 other neophyte student witches in training. What a huge change it was from the individual student classes and small coven of 3-4 people that we had only a year before. I could only start new groups as my schedule allowed- I had to juggle keeping my evening work to only certain nights of the week for the sake of my family and time with my husband. But it was working! The large majority of my students were excited, committed, and thrilled to be there. Over and over again each week I heard "this is the point I look forward to in each week", or "I'm so glad we get to come here and do this", or "I wish I had access to this type of magickal learning when I was younger". Most of my students stuck to the course and worked their way up to initiation. Of those, some were invited by me to continue on into Priesthood training, based on their aptitude and level of responsibility and investment through their training year.

I continue to have more and more people interested in the coven, and am working to become more and more of a positive public influence in the community. At this point, with the tried and true teaching structure in place and working well, and with other people being trained as teachers in the order, I feel confident that the Society of Witchcraft and Old Magick will continue on, even beyond my time, to perpetuate this tradition of American Witchcraft, even becoming its own subset of that tradition, and handing it on to future generations.

One of my clear and more recent spiritual callings has been to engage in acts of warriorship in honor of an ancient Irish Goddess that I work with. I was told through divine means that my role as a warrior is not in actual war in this life, but that my unique way of being able to risk myself for the benefit of others is through using my voice, teachings and example publicly to help disseminate thousands of years of built-up negative misconceptions around Witchcraft and make the way of the practice easier and more accepted for other pagans and Witches. So, I have been continuing to try to do things that keep me actively involved in that goal.

Becoming active at spreading awareness through our town's Halloween festivities, calling upon local journalism to support the spread of this message, helping authors to accurately portray modern day magick in their books, and attending pagan pride events are some of the things I've done so far to help spread the positivity and the inspiration that comes from the Craft. Writing this introductory book is another step I am taking in spreading this message of religious tolerance. It is definitely a challenge to get larger involvement from the coven itself to become active in community events and charitable work because of the need of many to remain incognito with regards to their status as a Witch. However, I will be looking for ways to show the community that our order can do a lot of good, and that modern-day witches are not to be feared the way that many years of patriarchal domination taught. Obviously blogging, and the publishing of this book is also a big part of that mission! And continuing to teach and ultimately find the others who will also one day teach will spread this work to more and more people in a way that is moral and respectful. I'm so proud of what I've managed to do with this coven so far. I'm constantly surrounded by groups of intellectually stimulating, magickal, intuitive, like-minded people. We support each other's magickal work and help each other make sense of all of the unique experiences of energy and consciousness that working with magick brings.

Back when I first decided to get formal training in the Craft, it was simply for me. It was because I had a passion for learning magick that I needed to feed. I never imagined that it would become my profession. I never imagined that the majority of my work week and income would come from running a real coven and magickal training school. I never imagined that people would also come to me for services professionally because of my magickal skills- I do professional tarot card readings, healing work, removal of negative entities, house clearings, handfastings, shamanic sessions, past life regressions, Ouija board classes and more, in addition to running the coven. I am a Witch. I am a bona-fide, modern day, formally trained, respected in the community, professional Witch, and Priestess. And if you read about the experiences I'm describing and compare them closely with some of the subtleties of magick that might have been bubbling around you in your life, you may just find that you are a Witch, too.

Part 2

What Makes a Person a Witch?

There is actually a lot of debate about this question in the magickal community. Many argue that to be a witch simply means that you identify with the role of a witch or immerse yourself in magickal practices. I don't disagree with this, but on the other side of the coin there are many people who feel that it is a title that is only earned through formal training and initiation. Certainly, in the tradition of my coven, a new student is called a neophyte, and one does not have the title of initiated Witch until after they have finished all of the requirements of the first year of training. I guess where people bump heads on it most is when self-proclaimed witches who are vocal on social media make claims that solitary practice is as effective as a traditional coven training in terms of bringing about the same levels of skill and knowledge. There seems to be a defensiveness there on the part of some who have chosen not to engage with a coven but still want to be seen as holding the same title and credibility as someone who has undergone formal training and initiation.

I can definitely say from my own personal, firsthand experience that I would never have achieved the level of depth of practice and scholarly approaches to learning that I have achieved, if I hadn't undergone formal training. There are many covens out there that do not have a structured curriculum or a longstanding tradition behind them, but if you are lucky enough to have access to one that does, the experience of going through the training is a lot like attending college. (Did I mention before that some of my students refer to my coven, the Society of Witchcraft and Old Magick as the "Yale of covens"?) Students who embark on a formal initiation program are required to attend weekly classes, full moons and sabbats, do homework, take quizzes and practice rituals at home so that they become adept enough to perform them for the group. It is a big commitment, but in taking that on, a person learns so much and has so many experiences that it does become hard to relate the earned title of initiated Witch to the self-proclaimed title. That being said, I never would deny someone their solitary title or their personal way of identifying with the Craft- I just like to be specific when it comes down to credentials. After all, credentials give you a concrete idea of someone's skill set- when someone has education and certification in a professional field such as nursing or accounting, for example, you know what that means, and you know they are qualified. The same actually goes for the field of witchcraft, believe it or not. For this reason, when I have to describe to someone what I do, I actually say I am "a formally trained and initiated Witch and Priestess" who now does yadda yadda, all of the things I mentioned above. This helps create a distinction between that level of achievement and the person who calls herself a Witch who has only read a couple of books and played around with herbs- now I am not belittling that, mind you, but there is a huge spectrum of experience and expertise that lies in the middle of this very varied spectrum.

Now, this title debate doesn't cover a third concept, and that is the idea of raw talent. There are many people who believe that you are either a witch by birth or not. This lies on the assumption that a witch is someone who is born with better-than-normal abilities in some area or areas. Now, you could argue that this is true in some ways. I normally find that most of my witchcraft students are more intuitive and empathic than the average Joe, and that it took a certain amount of intuition, courage and magick even to get themselves to the place of committing to this level of magickal training in the first place. On top of that, many of my students also have keen abilities in a specialty area such as communicating with the deceased, speaking to animals, projecting healing energies, doing psychic readings, or working with plant spirits just to name a few. I, myself had always been a pretty prophetic dreamer and had plenty of natural experiences with extra-sensory perception prior to my formal training as a witch, and then certainly upon training found more natural abilities in the areas of healing and psychic readings.

So again, yes- there are plenty of people out there who have certain "supernatural" traits that seem to be sharper than they are for average folks. I'm not sure if that qualifies you automatically as a witch- certainly not by everyone's definition. However, if you do have those raw skills then you may be predisposed to

witchcraft one way or another. Having a predisposition for something and choosing to cultivate that skill in a disciplined way, however, are certainly not the same thing. I'm sure I could have succeeded at any number of professions if I had chosen differently- I could have been a doctor, but I didn't choose that educational path and that practice, and so I don't call myself one. And there are certainly going to be some people who are born more predisposed to do witchcraft than others. Not everyone who tries will come to it as easily as the next person. I suppose we really need a solid definition for the modern-day idea behind the word "Witch" in order to say whether or not a person qualifies as one. The dictionary gives the definition of witch as: a person who professes to practice magic or sorcery. If we go by this, then raw talent by birth is not enough, it would require actual practice. There are a lot of people who read about the Craft and identify as a witch but don't really ever actually do anything. I know this from having heard the story from many, many people who were in that boat prior to joining my coven.
Even with practice, however, a self-proclaimed practicing witch and a formally initiated witch still imply different levels of experience and educational background. So, to answer the initial question of what makes one a witch...for me I would say it is having solid magickal study, experience and an ongoing personal magickal practice in witchcraft.

What do you believe is the spiritual nature of the universe? Are you driven by the magick of nature? Do you remember your dreams and have lots of psychic experiences? Is it easy for you to sense the energy in and around your body, or in other people or objects? Have you begun any studying of your own in the Craft? How do you currently define the word "Witch" in your own vocabulary? Notice if you have any feelings of either fear or inspiration when you think about it, and then ponder why that may be.

How Others Respond to You

One interesting thing to consider in wondering about your natural aptitude as a Witch is to study ways that people have reacted to you throughout your life. I can remember even as a child feeling as though many people would stare at me a little too long just walking through a mall or public place. I assumed they were being creepy until one day my mother remarked "people are naturally drawn to look at you". I realized then that it wasn't just creepy men or weirdos- it was that I exuded something that many people could sense- something a little more magnetic or energetic than the average person in a crowd. Even though the average person doesn't necessarily walk around seeing auras, people may be instinctively drawn to stare or do a double take when presented with someone who has a naturally strong energy field. But of course, I didn't understand all of this until much, much later. I remember numerous people describing me either to my mom or to my face as "sparkly". It's an interesting way to describe someone, no? If I chose that word to describe someone, it would have to be because they exuded a certain brightness of spirit, or something energetically attractive to others, because I wasn't walking around literally sparkling. Now I know that the people that I think of as sparkly have very strongly emanating auras with unique color frequencies in them….but I didn't know that back then, either.

I have also been told by a large number of people, very spontaneously, that they believed I was a fairy! This is a strange thing to hear over and over again. Some of those that said it were actual psychics and many were just random people who only had a preconceived notion of what a fairy is, not actual experience in fairy sighting. This means that there must be something about my overall look and energy that makes a person think this occasionally- again, it may be my energy field, with something that makes a person think of sparkles, which makes them think of fairies. I have also been told by psychics and some others the vague statement that I "am not from here", meaning I have an energetic type that seems alien, or that they believe my first incarnations were not actually of this earth. To me, any of it is possible. I don't limit my beliefs on things like that that you can't prove. I have had too many experiences of altered consciousness and other realities to assume that any less than anything is possible.

People will always respond to you from within the framework of their beliefs. An example of this happened when I was in my mid-twenties and was on a cruise that had a stop in Saint Thomas. I was strolling around in a cute little gift shop, looking at jewelry, and the shop owner, clearly an island native judging by her dress and accent, stopped and stared at me. There were plenty of other people in the store at the time, so it was odd for her to single me out so obviously. Then she said, "Girl, Jesus has an extra special love for you!". I was slightly taken aback, but just smiled and thanked her and made my purchase. I could tell by her eyes and the way that she looked at me that she was seeing something, and from her point of view, it seemed like a divine or Godly gift. I suppose that is what an extra sparkly aura would seem like to a person from that sort of faith! I was also told by a legally blind psychic that I was clearly different, and was a "Lightworker". These are some examples of remarks and experiences that, when I look back and add them all up, have been frequent throughout my life. I'm pretty sure that not everyone has had this trend, so if you have felt anything similar, or have noticed intermittent trends of people noticing unique otherworldly traits about you, you may have some special energetic talents, and maybe you should consider tapping into them!

Do people ever make odd or otherworldly remarks about you? What are the common first impressions of those who meet you? Do you often find yourself in social situations and feel like you are on the outside looking in? Do strangers come up to you out of the blue, feeling drawn to talk to you? Do strangers sometimes seem remarkably forward in telling you that you look a certain way? These are interesting experiences to consider when wondering if your energetic field stands out in a crowd.

What Do Modern Day Witches Believe, and What Do They Practice?

There are lots of different traditions of witchcraft and many styles of practice, so the belief system of the practicing witch can vary greatly from one person to the next. There are some witches who simply view magick as an energetic science and perform their work without any spiritual guidance or structured beliefs in place, but I think this is not what you'll normally find. Most witches, from what I see, do believe in something greater than themselves, similar to what is normally referred to as "God" in mainstream culture. The difference is that we do not tend to see God as one masculine personality who judges or who has set rules or agendas. Most witches tend to view the divine as being both masculine and feminine, mirroring the balance which exists in nature on the whole.

I tend to use the word "Spirit" instead of "God" to refer to the sum total of all the intelligent, creative energy in the universe. This is a huge concept which also hearkens back to the idea of "The All" in classical Hermetics. For me this implies that we are all included and connected within this concept of the Universe as one singular, expansive organism, as is every single thing you can imagine. Within the idea of Spirit, when I use the words "God" or "Goddess", I am referring to the intelligent divine masculine or feminine energies in nature, respectively. I also use those terms to refer to specific deities, or Gods and Goddesses, of various pantheons of world mythology. Many witches work exclusively with one pantheon of spirits such as Egyptian, Celtic, Greek, Vodou, etc, depending on their background or what they are simply naturally drawn to. American Witchcraft, my tradition, doesn't center around any one culture, but just like America itself, is a melting pot of ideas. We consider it just fine to learn from Odin as well as Isis, Buddha, Ganesh, Legba, Thor, Brigid and even Jesus to name just a few. I believe they are all connected to, and are aspects of the same source of infinite intelligent consciousness. Many witches also work with angelic and Saint energies, spirits of the deceased, and of course with the spirit energies of animals, plants and elements of nature. What I love about this and many other traditions of witchcraft is this openness, this willingness to explore multiple cultures and learn their magick, and to learn from their varied spiritual teachings and approaches. It certainly allows for greater acceptance of a wider variety of world cultures, and an expanded understanding of the interconnectedness of us all.

One area where there is a lot of discrepancy in terms of belief systems of witches is the area of ethical magickal behavior. Some witches believe that you should never do harm with your magickal abilities, some feel that it is okay only under certain karmically justified situations, and others have no problem shooting out hexes left and right. I fall in the middle. I've often been asked "Are you a white witch or a black witch?". I'll look into the eyes of the person asking and sense their fear level, but even if I can see that they are looking for one specific answer, I never just say "White!". I usually say, "I have extremely high ethical standards for my practice of magick." Everything lies on a spectrum, and hardly anything is all the way at its extreme end. In other words, every witch's practice, including my own, falls into some shade of gray, and saying anything other than that feels inauthentic to me.

Now, I am also fully aware that in some cultures, magicians hone their skills specifically to work either in the light or dark end of things. Even when this is the case, the person themselves, the quality of their spirit, their ethics, their emotional and mental backdrop is still always going to be in some shade of gray. Some shades are lighter or darker than others, obviously! I feel that at this point in my magickal career I understand all too well that there is always a balance- a balance in ourselves, in what we do, in nature around us, and in the Universe as a whole. The yin/yang symbol might be the most genius way to depict this that was ever created. You might be considering one end of the spectrum of light and dark, but there will always be a seed of its opposite neatly embedded within it, and within yourself, no matter what. My personal philosophy around so-called white and black magick is this: If you can achieve what you need to without doing harm, then that is the ethical thing to do. However, if someone is purposely harming you, you have the right to stop it. I have full respect for Jesus but I am just not a "turn the other cheek" kind of girl. I still probably would not be intending any harm, even with magick to bind or freeze someone's ill intent. Someone would have to be doing something pretty darn bad to me or my children for me to wish them harm, and I feel there are many ways to do magick where no harm is needed.

I think a great metaphor for understanding responsible magick lies in considering disciplined martial arts. If you learn a martial art you are taught self-defense, but you are also taught how to attack, maim, and hurt your opponent if need be. You are also taught to always hold a deep respect for the art, and that you always choose the most peaceful way out of a sticky situation, and only resort to your more damaging moves when absolutely necessary. This is how I think of the ethics of magick. I feel happy and empowered because I know I have many skilled options for protecting myself and banishing harm if I need to, but I don't abuse that power, and do my best to protect the innocent from harm whenever possible.

I certainly don't like when I see witches in social media flaunting photos of their hexing candle setups and accompanying them with phrases such as "someone's going to get theirs, hahahaha". Firstly, by having to share like that I feel they are trying to get validation of their own power. In other words, a truly capable witch would not feel the need to do that, and in fact, wouldn't want to for any risk of skeptical eyes on the setup potentially dissipating the strength of the work. Secondly, they are not helping the overall state of the social acceptance level of witchcraft by acting flippant about hexing. If we want to become treated with more respect as a real spiritual and religious societal group, we need to set a good example of morality that will stand up alongside the morality guidelines of the world's other leading religions. And while it irks me to see these people hexing too casually, I also don't like the "all love and light all the time" propaganda. There are a lot of people on social media who tout love and light nonstop. Okay, it's nice, and I get it. I get that you want to spread goodness and be a positive force. It's just that there definitely needs to be acceptance of darkness in the self and the world in order to have an understanding of just how much love and light you can exude. A person that holds a lot of fear of darkness, death, etc, isn't really projecting a ton of love and light- it is a wish at that point, more than a real force.

Also, people don't talk about the ethics of healing, but it deserves just as much karmic/dharmic consideration as hexing. We think that just because we are intending to do good, that it is ethical to exert our influence, but I disagree. When a student is taught Reiki, there is immense discussion about receiving specific permission from the intended recipient of the healing. There is also humility taught with respect to the idea that we cannot ever truly know what is in the highest and best interest of another. I believe it is unethical to pray for people in the way that many devout Christians will do, such as "Please Dear God, let (subject) stop smoking to preserve his/her health. Amen." The person praying for this cannot know what the consequences will be if their request is honored. If they stop smoking too soon, they might gain a ton of weight, or have their anxiety go through the roof and do something drastic, or any number of possible outcomes. It could also be great for them to quit right away, but the bottom line is that the smoker needs to be involved in that decision and knowing when and how it will be right to conduct it.

Even when I do magickal works of good, I stay aware that there is some kind of energetic cost for everything in magick, and that the recipient of the magick is ultimately the one doing any real healing. The witch or magician can set the stage, offer appropriate vibrations to be accessible and enlist spiritual help, but the recipient still needs to be the proper channel for the work. All magickal action requires close ethical scrutiny, whether seemingly light or dark, and often a banishing or a binding is a form of healing in and of itself. There will always be a natural balance hidden beneath the surface, so if there is a poor acceptance of one's darkness, primal power, relationship to death, etc, then the amount of light on the opposite end of that spectrum will be equally as dim. And I do believe that our current society's denial of and unwillingness to speak healthily about death is a huge problem that perpetuates fear unnecessarily. Well, now I digress, but let's just say that you'll probably see a whole separate book from me at some point on working with the vibrations of death to lessen fear and enhance the fullness of life.

The personal practices of witches probably vary even more greatly than their possible spectrum of beliefs. Many people, as I alluded to previously, identify with being a witch and read a lot but never really put much of anything structured into personal practice in terms of magick. This leads to being stuck in a constant state of longing for truly enchanted experiences that reside only in the mental realm and never manifest in the physical. (I should point out that "magick" as a term with a k on the end has come to be the understood term of use to denote the actual spiritual or metaphysical practices of magick, differentiating it from the normal spelling of "magic" in order to not have it be confused with entertainment or stage magic.)

And then there are many people who collect crystals, do some meditation and dabble with spells they have found in books. This is the average, middle of the road "witch" who does bring some magickal energy into physical life but may still be lacking deep profound experiences. For me, my practice is my life- meaning that I try to remember to hold an enchanted worldview all the time, even when doing something seemingly mundane. (There is something very satisfying about practicing a projection of positive energy when standing in line at the DMV!) I have immersed my entire life in the Craft since it became my job- I do daily ritual, teach the Craft to others, hold large coven gatherings for moons and Sabbats, and provide lots of healing work and magickal services to my community.

Teaching and Goddess devotion are certainly the aspects of my work that have deepened my personal practice the most. When I train students in the Craft I provide them with a well-rounded experience- a combination of scholarly lecture and study, ritual skill and attendance, and unique experiential sessions where they engage in various types of magick. This, of course, has me engaging in magick all of the time, with different combinations of people, and keeps me very vested in facilitating depth of experience for all involved. Obviously, not every witch is going to find his or herself in the position of teaching where this is the case, but it is still possible to structure ongoing experiences for oneself that allow further and further magickal exploration and skill. I have had teachers in the past who have said that there is nothing like teaching a topic to make you better at it, and they were right on.

Directly cultivating a relationship with a Goddess who strongly called to me has been another thing that has led to amazing magickal experiences for me, and has further formed my personal beliefs. At this point I am quite devoted to the Irish Goddess The Morrigan, and it will be difficult to describe how fulfilling this has been. Now, I don't feel limited in terms of being able to communicate and work with other guides and deities. You could say we have a sort of open relationship! Once I began reading about her, I couldn't stop. It just started with an ongoing interest, and a pull that kept me longing for more information. This led to a deepening sense of connection. I began to work past the superficial descriptions of her and into more scholarly works derived from the old original mythology. It chilled me to discover that dreams I had had in the past, encountering odd beings actually fit some of her descriptions, and in one dream she had even identified herself with a name which I now know to be one of the lesser known aspects of her.

I have since done rituals in honor of her, dedicated my workouts to the cultivation of her warrior aspect within myself, read more and more books, crafted oils, incantations, meditations, grimoire pages and more, in her name. In return, she has shown up in dreams, infused me with energies and experiences beyond belief, assisted me in my own magickal workings and also helped me to vanquish negativity whenever needed. I feed the crows in the neighborhood for her, and even have a large raven and moon tattoo on my leg that is dedicated to her. To some of you who are magickal newbies or haven't explored magick yet for yourself, this may all seem quite extreme, and I am well aware of that. I have had encounters with the Morrigan that I can only describe as true spiritual revelations. They make me understand the devoutness of many other people toward any religion.

Once you have personal proof of a divine force causing unimaginable experiences in yourself, that becomes an incredible motivating inspiration in life. It gives you a sense of understanding things across multiple planes of existence, as well as a sense of protection, power and deep kindred connection. Many modern-day Witches work with individual deities and guides in some of the ways that I have described from my own practice.

Aside from teaching and my own personal Goddess devotional work, some of the practices of the Craft that I engage in most frequently are dream work, shamanic energy healing, spell work, and divination, most often using the tarot. To me spells are practical applications of skills learned in the Craft, and they enhance one's manifestation abilities greatly. I have had great success with my spell work- both the ones I've done for my personal benefit, as well as those I've done on behalf of others. It is super empowering, and the results often start to be seen the very day of the casting. Many people think first of spell casting when they think of witches, but this is nowhere close to being my most important magickal tool.

Dream work is probably my greatest source of inspiration, magickal learning and spiritual connectedness. I have been paying attention to and journaling daily my dreams ever since I began as a student in the Religious Order of Witchcraft, and maybe randomly before that as well. In 2011, while working on my Master's degree in Integrative Health and Healing, I met Robert Moss. He is a prolific author and world renown shamanic dream teacher. He travels around the globe teaching his well-honed style of Active Dreaming to people of all walks of life. His mission is to move us back to becoming a dreaming society- that is, one in which dreams are highly valued, where they are looked to daily for guidance as well as for a source of knowledge on the infinite realms of reality in the multiverse, what comes after death, and where our deepest healing and spiritual connections lie.

When I met Robert and described to him my view on dreams and how I would incorporate them into my life's work, he invited me to attend his exclusive dream teacher training. Working with him and with world class dreamers from around the globe on my shamanic dreaming skills has been one of the most amazing and influential endeavors of my life. I proceeded to attend all three week long annual teacher trainings to move through his most advanced level of teacher training work. Each level brought more applications of dream work, more confidence in navigating non-ordinary reality to further explore the realms of dreaming, and more amazing experiences of synchronicity and magick.

To this day I continue to have an ever-expanding array of dream experiences that include frequent precognitive and divinatory dreams, dreams of healing and information that arise for me to give to others, dreams that teach me magickal skills and provide me with new techniques that transfer over into my practice in ordinary reality, and an increasing frequency of existence in the truly lucid dream state, where all things are possible and accessible. In the lucid dream state, or "conscious dreaming" as Robert prefers to call it, you can test theories, access the divine, move between realms at will, and much more.

One example of learning magick from a dream is as follows: I dreamt that I was driving around my town with an herbalist and healer friend of mine. We would identify stranded people who needed healing. (In the dream they would literally be laying alongside the road!) We would stop and get out and sit on either side of the person, and hold pink roses in our hands, cupped carefully. Using breath, we would inhale deeply, which caused the roses to levitate slightly and become all sparkly and obviously energetically infused, and then when we exhaled, the sparkling roses would dissipate downward into the heart center of the person being healed, absorbing into their chest and providing the healing needed in the moment.

Some time later, in ordinary reality, I was doing a typical Reiki healing session on a client. As the woman lay before me on the table, relaxed and with her eyes closed, I came around to the point where I would normally work on the heart chakra. Out of nowhere, this dream popped into my mind. Intuitively, I proceeded to flip my hands to an upturned, cupped position as they had been in the dream when holding the roses. I built up a clear vision of the roses being there, and then as I inhaled, I recreated the vision of the levitating, sparkly enlivening of the roses, and on the exhale I envisioned the integration of the rose magick infusing the heart chakra of my client. It felt nice, and I completed the session. When it was over and we were chatting afterward and comparing notes per the usual routine, my client exclaimed "I saw this beautiful pink rose and it merged into my heart!". I was stunned by this, as it validated the tangibility and the magick of the experience on all levels. I knew that bringing the technique of the dream to the session was a good idea when I was doing it, but I had no idea how immediate and clear the effect would be for the client. Ever since that experience, I have tried to make sure not to miss anything from the dreamtime that could translate into magick that I use here in this reality. The options are limitless. I am sure that there is also a book on dreaming that lies in my future publishing life, so I'll save the recounting of more specific stories from my explorations there for that work.

Another of my favorite magickal skills is reading the tarot. To describe how this has come to be such rewarding work requires a bit of an explanation of my take on divination itself. I don't do much divination for myself personally. The mind is a very powerful thing, and I feel that it is very difficult to be an accurate reader when you are too personally vested in the outcome. (And who is not vested in their own personal outcomes?) If you are watching a stilled pendulum and you ask a question and wait to see if there will be a yes or no response, your mind can actually influence the direction of the swing based on the strength of your desires, if you can't get them completely out of the way, which is hard to do. And with a tarot reading, you can twist the interpretation of the card meanings to better fit your hopes if you are not able to stay clear and unattached from the possible outcomes. If I do feel like doing a reading for myself, in order to avoid influencing the reading, I will choose to start with a "show me what I need to know" attitude. This leaves me to receive a reading based on advice, and not necessarily direct circumstantial outcomes as would be the case if you asked, "what will happen with this situation?", etc.

Anyway, I do perform a lot of tarot readings professionally for others, and they are incredibly rewarding both for myself and my clients. Whenever I sense fear of possible outcomes on the part of the client, I explain that I don't think everything we experience in life is completely scripted and fated. I believe that our own free will is always a tool and an influence on what we achieve. I like the way the Norse teachings speak of fate versus free will. I have heard it described in terms of a weaving loom. The vertical threads which are stabilized as the base of the piece are your structure, your underpinnings. They represent the facets of you that are innate to your spirit and your experience and are the things that will not change. The horizontal threads are where all of the options come in- you can choose different colors, patterns, and images and create the weaving as you go. These represent your volitional influence in life events- your free will and the choices you have acted upon. I believe that in a tarot reading we get to see the tendencies that exist energetically based on the client's state in the present moment.

A good reading will have both outcomes, thought processes and advice built in, to show that both circumstantial trends and free will are to be considered. I am always amazed at how accurately the cards will speak to the situation of the client. No matter how familiar I become with the process of card reading, I am still surprised when I find out after a reading just how on target it was. I chalk this up to the unconscious connection that is made when two people come together with a clear and joint intention to discern clarity, without skepticism, and with an open channel between them. I have often steered my readings to serve as a way for clients to best view their lives and their potential actions, rather than just worrying about what will literally happen, because a person needs to always take an active role in what will actually happen in their life, and this is key in the Craft. In this way, the cards have become a very therapeutic spiritual tool in my practice.

Shamanic practice, especially journeying, is another area of my personal brand of magick that is incredibly fulfilling and an ongoing source of deep, enchanting experiences. I had had some random experiences with shamanic style journeying at individual workshops, and had done some reading on the topic, but it wasn't until the combination of learning with Robert Moss as I mentioned above, and having the experience of training as a Shamanic Reiki Master practitioner with Llyn Roberts, that my skills in this area really took off. Those two mentors appeared to me in that same year that I was working on credits for my Master's degree in holistic health.

My experience with Llyn included a week-long training retreat where we learned to incorporate shamanic practices in with our already-existing Reiki skills. You wouldn't think lying around on yoga mats all day doing meditative activities would be tiring, but the task of completing numerous journeys on behalf of others per day was rigorous to be sure. Journeying is typically the act of turning one's attention inward, to an inner landscape of non-ordinary reality. From an established starting point, one usually travels in the mind's eye to another plane of existence, either as an exploration, or on a specific mission of working with or finding guides, receiving advice, or finding healing or assistance for oneself or another. Once mastered, the art of journeying can be used to augment almost any psychic, healing or personal growth work imaginable.

At this point, because I have practiced it so much and under so many different circumstances, I can pretty much do it on the fly. By this I mean that I can intentionally journey while standing, doing healing work on a client, or drumming for others.
Being able to do this and to trust the validity of the visions that come from it has helped me to develop in all other areas of psychic practice. For many people, developing that trust in one's inner self and inner landscape is the hardest piece of putting together a rewarding psychic practice.

Do you already engage in some of the practices or beliefs that are common to witchcraft? Which areas of magick are you drawn to learn more about? Have you always wanted to learn to read cards, or to understand your dreams? If you try to imagine right now what it would be like to have special psychic powers, what does that fantasy look like?

How to Speak to Skeptics or Naysayers About Witchcraft

Let's imagine now that you are interested in, or already have started studying witchcraft, but are afraid to talk about it to anyone. One of the toughest things about considering witchcraft as a part of your own life is the fear of having to explain yourself to those who still hold it in a very negative light. Even though we no longer live in an age where people are being actively sought out and killed for witchcraft, (at least in this country) the devilish definitions of the word "witch" and "witchcraft" as delineated by Christianity and perpetuated for two thousand years have left a huge scar behind. The thing is that modern witchcraft entails working with natural and spiritual energies, and for most practitioners, is an incredibly beautiful and moral way of life.

I used to keep my witchy ways completely secret- no one knew except for my husband and maybe one or two of my closest friends. When I could no longer stand to keep such an important part of myself hidden anymore, I began taking opportunities to mention it if an appropriate turn of conversation allowed. The results were amazing. The majority of the time, the person in front of me would be very accepting, touched that I trusted them, and very curious to know more. In the rarer cases where my honesty seemed to bring up fear in the person hearing about my witchcraft, there were still no negative consequences. If anything, being super honest and open about something like this teaches you what real, accepting relationships are. Why would you want any less? I feel that if people balk at my ways because they disagree or disapprove, then I've successfully filtered more judgment and false relationships from my life. Let's face it (and this is really hard)- if you have a relationship with someone now that would deteriorate if you told them you were into a moral practice of witchcraft, think about what that relationship is really based upon. They accept their imagined version of you, not the real, true version that seeks mystery and inspiration, and should be allowed to have religious freedom.

It is hardest for new practicing witches if the person they are afraid of telling is a family member. Even so, I have come to believe that there truly are no actual negative consequences to being authentic, open and honest about your beliefs and life motivations. A family member that really loves you is still going to, and one that only purported to love you because they felt they should may show their true colors. Having the truth about someone's feelings or judgments can only help you to conduct yourself accordingly, and to have healthy boundaries, in my opinion.

So, you're in a social situation with a friend. You are not sure how they would react to the idea of witchcraft, but they ask you what you have been up to lately. When witchcraft is the first thing that comes to mind and then you feel like you can't say it, it feels like lying. So, what do you say? Keep it honest, but simple. Be sure to be confident- if you seem nervous, that will make the other person feel like they have something to be nervous about too. Be sure to say things like "witchcraft is one of the many pagan earth/nature-based forms of spiritual practice". It always helps to mention that it has nothing to do with the devil (as long as that is true for you) and has its own code of ethics. I often say - "Just like Christians who believe in God, I do as well, it's just that I believe in God and Goddess as a reflection of the divine masculine and feminine throughout all of the natural world". I usually just leave it there for the listener who has any skepticism. For someone who is accepting and gets excited, I'll answer all of their follow-up questions honestly and happily.

It is very common, after telling someone that you study witchcraft for them to come right back with the very next question: "So, do you cast spells???!!!" I calmly smile and say "yes, but a spell is just a ceremonial form of prayer that brings in nature elements to augment it". Now, spellcasting can be pretty elaborate, and there are loads of things to consider, but virgin ears don't need to think about all of that. We just want them to understand the basic underpinnings so that they know who you really are. In fact, my first year magick students don't cast a fully timed, prepared formal spell until they are about three quarters of the way into their year of training- this is because they need to have a strong base in planetary magick, herbs, oils, crystals, Qabalah, astrology, divination, connecting to Spirit, ceremonial magick and more before the spell can be really well-executed. But the truth of the matter is that it still is a reverent and prayerful action- and that is all the skeptic needs to understand. Of course, you can chuckle and assure them that you don't sacrifice goats or babies and reiterate that your church is nature or any space you create as sacred for yourself.

If anyone has arguments to offer to any of these points, they won't hold water, and will be coming from a fundamentalist point of view. In other words, no one would be able to find fault with what you just described based on logic, so if they are still displaying fear or disapproval, it comes from formerly ingrained teachings that are specific to one religious tradition. Witches are generally open and accepting of all variety of world religions as being equally valid, and if you have to, you can point out that you would hope that in today's small world, you would love to think that others could see that point of view as well. Sometimes you can point out to people that you aren't doing any harm, so what is there to judge? And they will come back with a statement regarding how they are simply fearful for you because they think it is dangerous, or evil or bad for you. Assure your loved ones that you can and will take care of yourself. I think eating wheat is bad for you, but I'm not judging you for it.

Have you found yourself wishing you could talk about magick, witchcraft, paganism or psychic concepts with other people? Do you ever feel that you are unjustly restraining a very important and powerful part of yourself? Do you feel like there is an immense well of divinity and wisdom within yourself that is yet untapped? Are you tired of talking about politics and the weather, and wish you had people in your life with whom you could speak of psychic occurrences, the afterlife, dreams and the like?

Are You a Witch? Take the Quiz and Consider!

Okay now, keep in mind that this is just for fun! This quiz is not scientifically proven to be accurate and this is not a psychiatric measure of any kind. Even if your quiz score doesn't reflect the amount of witchiness you hoped you had, don't despair. You may be much witchier (or less if that's what you were hoping) and the quiz just isn't reflective for you. But if it is accurate, you can always work to become more magickal. The views are skewed and stereotypical and I admit it. But it's still fun to do. Write down the numbers one to twenty on a piece of paper, and then write the letter of your chosen response next to each for the twenty questions. When you have answered them all, go to the scoring chart at the end and add up your total. Then you can find your total in the categories of the witchiness descriptions that follow. Be honest, and enjoy!

1. You notice when it's about to be a full moon: a. Every month b. Once in a while c. Only if I look it up to figure it out d. Hardly ever e. Never
2. You remember your dreams: a. Every day b. A couple of times a week c. A couple of times a month d. Once in a long while e. Pretty much never
3. Choose a pastime: a. Hiking alone in nature b. Reading c. Watching movies d. Working out e. Travel
4. If you could redo everything and change my profession I would become a: a.

Doctor b. Yoga teacher c. Author d. Holistic healer e. Banker
5. You believe in: a. God b. Goddess c. Aliens d. Nothing unseen e. Everything
6. How many tattoos do you have? a. None b. The amount is no longer countable c. one pretty one d. Two or three e. I'm not telling
7. Which of these destinations would you go to specifically for shopping, if you could choose? a. Las Vegas b. New Orleans c. Salem, MA d. NYC e. Rodeo Drive
8. Choose one of the following to hang on your wall: a. Dried flowers b. Sword c. Nature Scenes d. Sigil of Protection e. Mirror
9. Which television program would you choose to watch right now? a. True Blood b. Mad Men c. Stranger Things d. Legion e. The Magicians
10. If you could choose one of these activities right now it would be: a. Receiving a high quality psychic reading b. Getting a massage c. Meeting friends for a walk d. Going to the department of motor vehicles e. Reading alone
11. Could you fathom wearing a pentagram in public? a. Never, I'd feel too uncomfortable b. I already wear one openly c. I'd only wear it with certain crowds or in certain places d. Yes but only if it's subtle and embellished with pretty crystals e. Yes, on Halloween
12. Which is your weapon of choice in the zombie apocalypse? A. Rifle b. My

husband c. Dagger d. Bow and arrows e. Sword
13. If you could have only one superpower, it would be: a. Flying b. Invisibility c. Shapeshifting d. Mindreading e. Super strength
14. When you start to feel like you are coming down with a cold you: a. Rest and hydrate well b. Go right to the doctor and lie about how many fevers you've had so you'll get antibiotics right away c. Load up on vitamin C d. Get a reiki session and drink chaga tea e. Whine and have your significant other wait on you
15. Your personal psychic experiences include: a. Occasional deja vu or esp b. Being able to sense the emotions of others c. Sensing the energy or awareness of a deceased spirit d. All of these e. None of these
16. Your favorite color is: a. Black b. Purple c. Blue d. Pink E. Green
17. Choose a landscape: a. Ocean b. Mountains c. Forest d. Desert e. Grassy fields
18. You believe in: a. Reincarnation b. Open to all the possibilities c. Heaven and Hell d. Nothing exists after death e. It's all just a dream
19. Someone you don't really know well starts badmouthing you on the internet. You: a. Get upset and spew some insults back b. Block them from being able to comment on your stuff and forget about it c. Consult your magickal friends

to see how you can best rectify this negative energy d. Hire someone to do a spell on your behalf e. Do nothing
20. You can envision yourself: a. Incorporating magick and the Craft into many aspects of your life b. Having fun reading and learning about magick c. Going to an occasional holistic workshop d. Desiring learning magick but being afraid to actually dive in e. Dabbling here and there

Okay, now look at your paper with your responses on it, write down the corresponding number amount from each question's response as indicated below, and add them up.

1. a. 5 b. 4 c. 3 d. 2 e. 1
2. a. 5 b. 4 c. 3 d. 2 e. 1
3. a. 5 b. 4 c. 3 d. 2 e. 1
4. a. 2 b. 3 c. 4 d. 5 e. 1
5. a. 2 b. 4 c. 3 d. 1 e. 5
6. a. 1 b. 5 c. 3 d. 4 e. 2
7. a. 1 b. 4 c. 5 d. 3 e. 2
8. a. 3 b. 4 c. 2 d. 5 e. 1
9. a. 4 b. 1 c. 3 d. 2 e. 5
10. a. 5 b. 2 c. 3 d. 1 e. 4
11. a. 1 b. 5 c. 3 d. 4 e. 2
12. a. 2 b. 1 c. 4 d. 3 e. 5
13. a. 3 b. 2 c. 5 d. 4 e. 1
14. a. 4 b. 2 c. 3 d. 5 e. 1
15. a. 2 b. 3 c. 4 d. 5 e. 1
16. a. 5 b. 4 c. 2 d. 1 e. 3
17. a. 4 b. 3 c. 5 d. 1 e. 2
18. a. 4 b. 5 c. 2 d. 1 e. 3
19. a. 2 b. 3 c. 5 d. 4 e. 1
20. a. 5 b. 3 c. 2 d. 1 e. 4

Okay, once you've got your score, look to see which category your number total falls into, and read the description!

1. (Scores from 20-35 points) <u>Cautiously Curious</u> : You have a little bit of witchiness bubbling up in you just based on the fact that you've picked up this book and taken this quiz, but you are still staying on the outskirts of this mystical field. You are developing an openness and an understanding of those around you who may have these interests, but they haven't yet seeped into your own day-to-day life. The great thing is that it's never too late to learn more! Keep reading all of the magickal literature you are drawn to and have an open mind and heart and your path will become more and more clear.

2. (Scores from 36-51 points) <u>Witchlet in the Making</u>: You've sensed occasional sparks of inspiration or thrill with respect to witchcraft and the occult. You're the type that loves horror and witchy movies and wouldn't balk at having your cards read. There is no better time than now to begin to acclimate more to nature and enliven your own natural psychic and intuitive abilities, because there is most certainly some talent there waiting to be discovered. See if you can start paying attention to dreams (or trying to remember them!), noticing synchronicities

in your life, and paying attention to things that seem like signs. You are on the precipice of magick!

3. (Scores from 52-67 points) <u>Your Magickal Traits are Starting to Show</u>: Those that know you probably would not find it surprising at all if they found out you had an interest in witchcraft. Your intuition is keener than that of the average bear, you are not afraid to arm yourself with the right metaphysical jewelry, and you know your way around Salem a little too well. Your underlying feeling that you have a predisposition for being good at magick is correct. If you haven't already, it is time to do some serious study and start to practice at home. Pick up a good book on practicing as a solitary witch in private and really do it- try all the practice meditations and journeys, follow the instructions to bless your tools and stones, and start to be aware of how the lunar cycle and seasons are affecting you. You won't regret it!

4. (Scores from 68-83 points) <u>Witchcraft is Your Secret Power</u>: You already have quite a lot of magick oozing from your pores. You've probably read your share of books and tried a number of spells. Your magick and your connection to the divinity in nature inspires you and lifts you from tough times, but you occasionally have this nagging feeling that you need

something more. If you haven't already, consider checking out the witchvox or paganspace websites, or any other such social site for meeting other pagans and witches. When you start to share your magick with others, allowing more openness and authenticity to come forth, your magick will blossom and strengthen even further. You will start to feel the fulfillment you've been looking for.

5. (Scores from 84-100 points) <u>You Belong in a Coven</u>: You are just about as witchy as they come! You are not shy about your level of magickal belief and living, and you've probably amassed a good amount of magickal information at this point. Whether you are for or against the idea of formal training in the Craft, don't rule it out. You may not know it now, but finding a high integrity, structured coven situation could be the thing that catapults you and your abilities to unexpected levels. You've already practiced with tarot, cast spells and more, so it's time to have your experiences fully validated in group practice. Better yet, with your natural tendencies you may be able to teach the Craft to others one day. Thank you for helping to preserve and pass on the wise ways of our ancestors!

Parting Words

Thank you for taking the time to read my ramblings. I'd love to reiterate what my goals were in sharing this book. The reason for sharing some of the memoir-style happenings of my life was to show how threads of magick and psychic ability can be present even in the most seemingly normal person's life. I meant to illustrate that this magick can blossom in you or anyone, if cultivated, no matter how "normal" or non-magickal your life appears from the outside. I also meant to show that a moral person, living an upstanding life can be guided to the ways of witchcraft without being on a power trip, being swayed by evil, or getting mixed up in a bad crowd. There are still far too many people who have fears like this, and it is one of my missions in life to help dissipate them so that Witches, Wiccans, pagans and all magickal practitioners have better acceptance, and experience more religious tolerance and equality. Lastly, I wanted to give a general overview of the practices and beliefs that are common to modern-day Witches to further the understanding of the general public. I am guessing that there will be certain types of people who will have read this book: one is the type who is curious and wondering if they have innate witchy tendencies, another will be those who are just simply interested in reading about another witch's life, and the last (I hope) will be those who have a little fear, or want to understand witchcraft better so they can accept others more openly. Regardless of whether or not you fit into one of these categories, any inspiration or increase in open-mindedness that results from this book will have made it a success in my eyes. I have a lot of other works I would like to publish, and I hope that we can make this witchcraft journey together, but for now, this is my introduction, my "hello" to the wider literary audience of the witchy and the witchcraft-curious. I wish you many blessings, and a lifetime of learning, love and inspiration. Blessed Be!

Bibliography of Mentions

Buckland, Raymond, *Buckland's Complete Book of Witchcraft*, St. Paul: Llewellyn, 1998.

Cabot, Laurie, *Power of the Witch: The Earth, The Moon, And The Magical Path To Enlightenment*, Crystal Lake IL: Delta, 1990.

Cunningham, Scott, *Wicca: A Guide For The Solitary Practitioner*, St. Paul: Llewellyn Publications, 1988.

Curott, Phyllis, *Book of Shadows*, New York: Harmony, 1998.

Grossman, Lev, *The Magicians*, New York: Viking Press, 2009.

Harkness, Diane, *A Discovery of Witches*, New York: Penguin Group, 2011.

Rowling, JK, *Harry Potter and the Sorceror's Stone*, New York: Scholastic Corporation, 1998.

Rice, Anne, *The Witching Hour,* New York: Ballantine Publishing, 1991.

About the Author

Nikki Wardwell Sleath grew up in Reading, Massachusetts and went on to study at the University of Connecticut and The Graduate Institute, earning a BS in physical therapy and then an MA in Integrative Health and Healing. She is a formally trained Witch and Priestess, and the founder and High Priestess of the Society of Witchcraft and Old Magick, whose headquarters is located in Collinsville, CT. She is also a Reiki Master/Teacher, Shamanic Reiki Master Practitioner, certified shamanic dream teacher, certified hypnotherapist, certified medicinal aromatherapist, and certified auriculotherapist. She is married with two children, and works full time running the coven and its magickal training school, conducting professional readings, spells, healing sessions, and writing.

societyofwitchcraft.com
nikki@nikkisnature.com

On facebook , the author can be found as Nikki Wardwell Sleath, and administering to the facebook pages Nikki's Nature and Society of Witchcraft and Old Magick.

Made in United States
North Haven, CT
01 March 2024